AESOP,
JUST
IN RHYME

5554-MURP

AESOP,
JUST
IN RHYME

A new, humorous version
of the great fables
for readers of all ages.

John W. Murphy

5554-MURP

To order additional copies of this book, contact:
Xlibris Corporation
1-888-7-XLIBRIS
www.Xlibris.com
Orders@Xlibris.com

CONTENTS

For Rita

5554-MURP

ABOUT AESOP:

It is believed that Aesop was born about 620 B.C. in Phrygia, located in present-day Central Turkey, but the Island of Samos has also been called his place of birth. He was twice a slave but was set free.

As an ambassador of the legendary King Croesus, King of Lydia, also part of modern-day Turkey, on the Aegean Sea, he went to Delphi. He was to present money from the King to the Delphians but an argument took place and he refused to do so. He was thrown from a precipice to his death.

No one knows how many of the Fables he actually told. They were not written down. It is possible that fables by others are attributed to him. But he is the acknowledged Master of this brilliant method of depicting human flaw.

The Tortoise and the Hare

"I'm by far the fastest, I'm the best,
I can beat you and all of the rest,"
bragged the proud hare to the gathered crowd
of beasts who were well-used to the loud,
rude boasting of this neighborhood whiz.

The peaceful tortoise spoke to the hare,
"A race between us, if you will dare,
would favor you with those who may bet,
but somehow I believe I can get
the better of you."

"Ha,ha," laughed the hare, "All will agree
that you're as fast as a wingless bee,
I'll run around you for half an hour,
still have time for a nap and shower."
The tortoise said, "We'll see."

They started on a challenging course,
the hare went zooming like a race horse,
paused for his nap to show he was great,
the tortoise moved at a woeful rate,
but went on and on.

The hare slept longer than expected,
his claim to greatness was rejected;
when the tortoise crossed the finish line,
the losing hare's boast became a whine.
Steady wins again.

Some Have It

At the yearly Animals' Talent Review
an artistic monkey danced to wild applause,
the audience screamed, begged him to continue
but, being breathless, squeaked, "I request a pause."

A camel, envious, sought recognition;
he knew he couldn't dance, so he sort of swayed,
made such a ridiculous exhibition,
he had to run quickly or would have been flayed.

A desire to perform
won't help if you have bad form.

Things Can Always Get Worse

Each morning the servant girls, in a heap,
were torn from their heavenly, blissful sleep
by their mistress who put them on their toes
as soon as she had heard the rooster's crows.

Feeling overworked beyond endurance,
shrewdly they gave themselves the assurance
that the only way to avoid their wreck
was to squeeze the old rooster by the neck.

They thought that with the noisy rooster gone,
they would sleep in peace until after dawn,
but their mistress woke them even earlier,
not only that, but she got surlier.

The quick answer may not be the best,
take time, look carefully at the rest.

5554-MURP

The Right Decision

A sleeping lion was quite disturbed
by a mouse that ran all over him.
The lion declared, "This must be curbed
or my chances for sleep will be slim."

He held the mouse, opened his large jaws,
planned to swallow the little fellow,
but the mouse's soft pleas made him pause,
changing his mood from angry to mellow,

"King Lion, pardon, I won't forget,
helping others is my best feature,
let me go and my help you shall get."
"GO!," laughed the lion, "You silly creature."

Later, the lion was caught, tied tight,
a wagon came to take him away
when, round the bend, the mouse came in sight,
the little hero would save the day.

He chewed the ropes, teeth sharp as a knife,
The King knew he had not made a boast,
they both agreed to be friends for life,
they skipped away, heading for the coast.

If, to all creatures you are kind,
they'll show you their talents, you will find.

17

First Things First

A boy dived in, swam far out one morning,
in spite of a sign that gave him warning
that the water was deep, the tide was strong,
and he was shouting, "Help me," before long.

A man on the bank called, "You foolish lad,
you should be punished for judgement so bad."
The boy yelled, "Save me now, keep in store
your lecture, until I am safe on shore."

For those who take pleasure in censure,
try helping, it's a new adventure.

Plan Ahead

Thinking life was fine, all was swell,
a careless fox slipped, fell into a well.
Unable to get out, he was stuck
till a goat came by, a stroke of luck.

"How's the water?" the goat asked, looked down,
"You'll love it," smiled the fox, "Best in town."
The goat jumped in, drank, then looked about,
questioned, "Tell me, how do we get out?"

"Not a problem for us, not at all,
put your forelegs high against the wall,
I'll climb up over you, I'll be out,
then I'll help you, don't you have a doubt."

The fox climbed to the top and was free,
the goat said, "What happens now to me?"
The fox advised, "Don't worry, you'll learn,
I figured it out, now it's your turn."

Trusting others is not a bad trait,
but it doesn't hurt to evaluate.

Mother and Son

A crab watched her son walk by the bay,
called, "Stop moving sideways, fix your walk."
The amused son smiled, "Show me the way,
give me your example, not just talk."

The mother took her son's words to heart,
practiced each day most vigorously.
She told him, after many a start,
"Son, that's the way it was meant to be."

Some mothers prove by their generous giving,
"The unexamined life is not worth living."

The Shepherd Boy

Below the mountains, sitting at rest,
a shepherd boy thought, "How can I best
find some friends?" He came up with a plan
and quickly to the village he ran,

Crying, "WOLF! Please help me," very loud,
was soon surrounded by a large crowd.
They saw nothing but gave him the doubt,
warned, "Be sure there's a wolf if you shout,"
and the boy was happy.

A few days later, again lonely,
the boy smiled, "It's easy, I've only
to shout, 'Wolf, Wolf ', and they'll come to me."
They came but there was no wolf to see,
and they were not pleased.

Turning homeward to tend his flock,
the boy looked ahead, then froze in shock
when he saw a big, grey wolf approach,
without doubt hungry enough to poach,
and he was afraid.

The boy called "WOLF," as loud as he could
but no folks came as he thought they should,
they thought that this call was not for real,
the wolf attacked and had a good meal.
And the boy sat down and cried.

23

The Cat and the Birds

A cat heard what to him was good news,
that a family of birds was ill,
"I'll pretend to have a doctor's skill,"
he said, and started to plan a ruse.

He found shirt, collar, long coat of blue,
taking great pains to play the part,
knocked at the birds' door and made his start,
"I'm a doctor, I'm here to cure you."

The birds chirped, "Thank you from one and all,
we're feeling fine, we don't get sick much,
why not leave your card and stay in touch
but don't hang out waiting for our call."

Dressing up may be your bent,
but don't think you'll hide intent.

5554-MURP

Extra Motivation

"WOOF, WOOF, here I come," howled the dog at the hare
as he flushed him from a bush behind a tree,
the hare hopped away with a speed rather rare
and the dog, losing ground, sadly watched him flee.

"HA, HA," laughed a shepherd, "I find that you're slow,
the hare is too fast," he said with insistence.
"Oh, I'm fast too, he's more motivated though,
the hare runs fast to continue existence."

When your life's at stake,
you don't need to brake.

Dolphins Whales and a Sardine

From early morning until the night,
the whales and dolphins pursued a fight.
When the battle was just at its height,
a pesky sardine came into sight.

He begged the combatants to do right,
"I can help you to see wrong is might."
The whales and dolphins didn't bite,
squealed, "Beat it shorty, go fly a kite."

Leave ill enough alone,
some may resent your tone.

Lion's Work

Being unemployed, having no pride,
a fox met a lion and applied
for the job of finding lion's prey,
and the lion would pounce every day.

As time passed by, the fox became bored,
he resolved to ask his lion-lord
if he could grab some prey, as a test,
the friendly lion roared, "Be my guest."

Next day the fox saw a flock of sheep,
he sneaked up close, did not make a peep,
the shepherd captured him as he whined,
"I'm out of work and I may be fined."

Ambition alone is not a good guide,
to move up, be sure you are qualified.

The Kite and the Pigeons

The Great Pigeon Congress met to talk
of the scary sighting of a kite,
so frightened they voted, "Ask the hawk
to banish this strange threat with his might."

They welcomed the hawk to their big coop,
confident that he'd be their savior,
but he placed several in a fine soup,
shocking all with his crude behavior.

Of your illness be sure
before you seek a cure.

29

Regret

On a lovely, sunny summer's day,
a proud grasshopper was heard to say
to a tired ant, bearing some corn,
"You look sweaty, weak and so forlorn,

"Why not come along to play with me,
we'll have lots of fun, just wait and see."
But the ant persevered at its task,
advised, "Dear grasshopper, you should ask,

"Where you'll get some food when cold days come,
my family will eat as you grow numb."
Grasshopper laughed, " I have much to eat,"
as the ant moved slowly in the heat.

Winter came, grasshopper found out too late
that planning and working must not wait,
he was cold and hungry, begged for food
while the ants ate in a happy mood.

Wolf and Goat

Looking down from the roof of a house
a goat shouted to a wolf below,
"You're a wretch, a thief, how dare you show
your face, you rascal; did I add 'louse'?"

The wolf looked up and scornfully stared,
"How odd," he grumbled, "How very strange
that you're so bold when out of my range;
but we'll soon be close, with my teeth bared."

Be careful of the seeds you sow,
when you're not looking, they will grow.

Eagle Scout

A farmer, walking to breathe fresh spring air
found a struggling eagle, caught in a snare,
alone and helpless. It seemed only right
to help it soar high in majestic flight.
He let it go.

The eagle, on a crisp, bright day in fall
saw the farmer sit by a crumbling wall,
flew straight down and snatched his jacket,
was chased by the man, making a racket,
and the eagle dropped it.

The man returned to the scene of the raid,
he suddenly knew he'd been repaid
with a kindness that seemed only fitting;
the wall had fallen where he'd been sitting.
He waved his thanks.

It's fun to savor
doing a favor.

The Idle Crow

An idle crow, unhappy with his lot
decided to be what he was not,
added peacock feathers to his own,
sought a high status, to most unknown.

His peers mocked him and sent him packing,
he fled to Peacock Lane, but lacking
the feathery beauty peacocks require
and soon they tossed him in the mire.

Then they sent him to Crow City
but the crows would not grant him pity,
"You decided we're not your equal,
for you, here, there can be no sequel."

Try not to be uppity, like the crow,
or your friends may say, "Time for you to go."

5554-MURP

Leadership

The mice and the weasels were at war,
the weasels were winning more and more,
so the mice decided they would seek
better leaders who were not so meek.

Each general put horns on his head
to show that the mice were bravely led
by commanders, of all mice the best,
far superior to all the rest.

Mice and weasels began the campaign,
the weaker mice retreated in pain
to their holes in a terrible rout,
but the generals' horns kept them out.

As they were captured, without a fight,
a wise old mouse stated, of their plight,
"Dress yourself up to be great
and you may find a fearsome fate."

The Stag That Fell Ill

A sleek stag, lucky to live at ease,
had his own pasture, all that would please,
life seemed his every wish to fulfill
but suddenly he fell very ill.

His many friends came to soothe his mind
but ate the grass, left desert behind.
When the stag's health began to improve,
his pasture, barren, forced him to move.

If your friends are coming, by the bunch,
remind each one to bring a good lunch.

5554-MURP

Dog in the Manger

A pampered dog with no job assigned
cruised the barnyard, hoping to find
a cool and sheltering place to creep
and spend the whole afternoon asleep.

Having searched most buildings on the way,
the dog ruled out the chance of danger
on fine hay in the ox's manger
since the poor, old creature worked all day.

The ox returns from a long day's tasks,
sees the dog at ease and mildly asks
the dog to move, to get at some hay
but the dog barks loudly, bars the way.

The ox declares, "You know it's my right,
after working, to have my dinner."
The dog growls, "Come nearer and I'll bite."
The ox says, leaving, "You're the winner."

Keeping from others what's of no use to you,
is one of the meanest things that you can do.

The Little Gnat and the Big Bull

A proud gnat, certain of his nuisance power,
landed quite gracefully on a large bull's back,
he buzzed and moved around for about an hour,
wondering how a beast could stand his attack.

"Am I bugging you too much, have I been fair?"
he asked the bull. "Heaven knows, I've just started."
"It's you," the bull yawned, "Didn't know you were there."
The gnat, deflated, left for points uncharted.

Be slow to praise your own influence,
just try to use some common sense.

The Horse and the Donkey

Side by side, a war horse and a donkey
sauntered along as the donkey opined,
"Your trappings are beautiful, I can see
your work is easy, you have peace of mind."

The horse spoke, "Yes, you have a heavy load
and I a very light one, that is true,
but war is horror, a terrible mode ,
what is perfect hangs on your point of view."

Next day in a fierce battle, the horse fell.
Wounded, near his end, he had no more fight.
The donkey chanced by, paused, had time to tell
the horse, "I'm sorry to say, you were right."

Before you dare wish to change places,
put yourself through the other's paces.

Invitation Declined

An aging lion lay in a cave,
too weak to hunt or to win in fights,
his days of glory and being brave
were now memories during cold nights.

But he was smart and figured it out,
he could still get enough food to eat
by giving visitors a big clout
and eating them while still in his seat.

A neighborly, wise fox came to call,
but remained a distance off to see
if all visitors were standing tall
long after they gave their sympathy.

When the lion called, "Please come inside,"
the fox knew his answer, without doubt,
"No thanks, I see many tracks go in,
but there are no tracks that come back out."

If you believe a visit will be hard,
perhaps it's better just to send a card.

The Wolf and the Guard Dog

A small, hungry wolf, roaming at night,
chanced to meet a splendid, healthy hound,
"You look well-fed, my friend, a rare sight,
do you know where some food might be found?"

"Eat from my bowl." The wolf ate, gave thanks.
"It's part of my pay, all I can eat,
to guard my master from crooks and cranks;
he leaves me free to patrol our street.

"If you like, perhaps you can patrol,
it's a good job, quite easy, you'll see."
"Sign me!" said the wolf, "Easy's my goal."
Then he heard, "You get a collar, FREE!"

The wolf balked, "A collar, that sounds hard."
"I'm chained all day, it's part of the deal,
'cause neighbors fear us." The wolf smiled, "Pard',
no chains, please. So long, thanks for the meal."

Work is good but be careful to see
that there is not a loss of liberty.

5554-MURP

. . . Now Walk the Walk

A young man known as a poor athlete,
returned from The Great Games, held in Crete.
He bragged how he had become a star,
beating all who tried to jump so far.

"I made the longest jump, had no peer,
ask the viewers if they come here."
A villager laughed, "To make your case,
jump right now, we have plenty of space."

Those who lie to get attention,
soon do not receive a mention.

When Dogs Meet

A dog with a piece of meat in his jaws
was crossing a bridge but soon made a pause,
saw his reflection in water below
and instantly stated, "It must be so,

"It's another dog with lots more of meat,
I think I'll jump down and get his to eat."
He attacked his image, fell in the bay,
knew his fault as his meat floated away.

Enjoy what you have, don't be greedy
or you may be classified, 'needy'.

5554-MURP

Polite Society

The Head Wolf announced a new law for the pack,
"We'll all set down what's caught in a common place,
no more eating each other, for none will lack
good food, there'll be plenty to feed every face."

An old wolf said, "To me, that sounds good and fair,
I certainly do not want to be eaten,
but when will you bring out, for us to share,
the big buck you caught and then hid in your den?"

When those in power offer largess,
Chances are they get more, we get less.

Monkey Afloat

A kind man with a monkey for a pet,
took him to sea on a vacation trip,
a fierce storm arose and soon all were wet.
The ship, near Cape Sounion, took a grave dip.

A dolphin saw the monkey couldn't swim,
offered him a ride and they were banded.
He thought the monkey a man, carried him
to Port of Piraeus, where they landed.

The dolphin asked, "You know Piraeus, then?"
(The monkey thought he referred to a man,)
smiled, "A friend of mine, a real prince of men,
I'll introduce you to him when I can."

Now the dolphin knew that the monkey lied
and thought he wasn't a real man, as well,
he was so angry and so mortified,
he pushed the beast into a rising swell.

To avoid wear and tear,
choose your new friends with care

A Doctor's Prescription

A patient's demise was a doctor's concern,
he told the relatives that, "We can all learn
from this tragedy. Our friend, as we look back,
could have avoided this sudden heart attack.

"He should have given up drink, eaten better,
had more workouts, sleep, all this to the letter."
A friend asked, "Doctor, forgive me if I'm rough,
when he lived, why didn't you tell him this stuff?"

Doctors, be nice,
give early advice.

In Good Time

Walking and searching by an old oak tree,
a starving fox saw in its small hollow,
some leftover food, went in to swallow,
and wolfed all of it down most hungrily.

With his stomach full, he couldn't get out.
A friend came by, looked down and said, "Bad luck,
keep calm, patience is the key here, not pluck,
sit back until you are no longer stout."

Who thinks before he jumps
will, perhaps, avoid lumps.

5554-MURP

Belling the Cat

The High Council of Mice met one fine day
to hear news about a frightening cat,
how they would avoid it and things like that,
so they wouldn't worry at work and play.

One bold young mouse shouted, "The problem's cause
is the sneaky manner the cat employs,
creeping up on us all, the girls and boys
and pouncing swiftly with those ugly paws,

"I propose to you all, (pardon my smarts)
that we put a ribbon on the cat's neck,
attach a big bell that will ring like heck
and we'll all hear the attack, if it starts."

"Brilliant," agreed the members, standing tall,
except for one mouse who quietly asked,
"Which one will bell the cat, who will be tasked?"
Slowly and sadly they all left the hall.

Some puff themselves up to make a suggestion
but doing the job is out of the question.

A Sad Tail

When a fox made a mess of a wheat field,
the farmer spoke, " I can't put him in jail,"
but he caught him and meanly made him yield
to having a fire set to his tail.

The fox ran fast to put the fire out,
he leaped to the farmer's field of ripe corn.
By the time he had completed the rout,
the crop was burnt and the farmer forlorn.

When in a crisis, pick a solution,
But please be sure it's not retribution.

Wind and Sun

" I'm much stronger than you are, this is no jest,"
growled The North Wind but The Sun did not concede,
he merely smiled, "Put this dispute to a test,"
and quite readily did The North Wind accede.

The Wind eyed a man in a coat, far below,
"Let's see who can remove it, do you agree?"
The Sun nodded, "Yes," the Wind began to blow,
the man buttoned his coat most rapidly.

When freezing winds howled, the man held the coat tight.
Vexed, the Wind saw victory slipping away,
"I'll rest a while, then I'll continue the fight,"
turning to the Sun, "I invite you to play."

Out shot a sunbeam, the buttons came undone;
Next, oppressive heat and soon off came the coat.
As the Wind nodded to admit who had won,
The Sun, a true sportsman, did not even gloat.

If you want people to come to your side,
be open and warm, or have a rough ride.

A Rabbit in Hand . . . .

Coming upon a rabbit asleep,
a lion thought, "An excellent meal!"
But when he saw a stag run and leap,
said, "That seems to be a better deal."

He chased the stag but was much too slow,
he returned to have a rabbit lunch;
the noise made the rabbit run and go,
the lion was left with scraps to munch.

Secure the dream at hand
before all turns to sand.

Eyes Right

A rich, old lady whose sight was poor,
called a certain doctor, well-renowned,
she promised a large fee for a cure
and daily, with charm, he came around.

She'd close her eyes, he'd place a compress,
tell gossip, her awareness to quell,
steal choice items she did possess
and assure she'd soon see very well.

He gave his bill, she declined to pay,
they went before a judge at claims court.
"I'm not cured sir, to this very day,
I'll not pay him nor those of his sort.

"Beginning treatment, (That day I curse),
I could see my treasures, every one.
Now, I believe my eyes are much worse
because I can't see a single one."

A new doctor may be in order
if all you own has crossed the border.

The Shepherd Explains Nature

While minding his flock of sheep by the shore,
a shepherd, enthralled by the placid sea,
had the sudden thought that he could earn more,
buying and selling cargo, for a fee.

He borrowed some money, against his flock,
rented a ship and bought all kinds of fruit.
Off he sailed but the ship began to rock,
and a startling storm made him change his route.

The storm got worse, cargo had to be tossed
to save the old ship from going under.
Returning to port, cargo and sheep lost,
he was broke and broken, (What a blunder!)

Again by the sea, a stranger passed by,
asked him, "The water's calm, caused by heat?"
"Oh, no, I don't think so," was his reply,
"It's telling us it wants more fruit to eat."

If you take weird courses,
don't blame outside forces.

Bad Nanny, Good Nanny

Looking out for some stomach-filler,
a hungry wolf passed a cottage door.
A nanny shouted like a killer,
"Hush, I'll throw you to a big wolf, or

something worse." The child, not excited,
had heard that sort of thing more and more,
but the wolf outside was delighted,
thought, "This is what I've been waiting for."

He sat all day below the window,
hoping, praying the nanny would act,
but nothing happened, it was all show,
nanny and child lived a secret pact.

At night, the nanny said, "I love you,
if a wolf appears, we'll beat him up."
Wolf said, "If I were human, I'd sue."
He went home, as helpless as a pup.

Interpreting human emotion
can cause your brain lots of commotion.

Grave Monkey

Two travelers debated at great length,
their ancestors' high station and their strength
of character, how perfect were their mates,
and the splendid glory of their estates.

They walked by a site of majestic tombs,
the monkey wept long, the fox asked, "What looms?"
"Think," said the monkey, "When I end life's race,
with my royal clan, I will have a place."

"Noble thought," mocked the fox, "That you pretend,
this joke of yours may never have an end,
who lies here won't contradict what you say,
none has the power to rise and shout 'NAY'."

Those whose pleasure is to pretend
are often alone in the end.

5554-MURP

His Own Fault

A horse and a donkey were on a road,
their Master gave the donkey a big load
which resulted in damage to his heart,
so he asked the horse, "Won't you take a part?"

But the horse said proudly, "You are confused,
a horse is not a beast to be abused."
The donkey moved slowly, collapsed and died,
the horse felt no pity but soon lost his pride,

As the Master switched the load to his back,
plus the donkey's hide, he thought he would crack.
Now a beast of burden, he saw too late
that selfishness had caused his sorry fate.

If only some kindness you'll extend,
you may save yourself and make a friend.

The Master Speaks

"Oh, Master Aesop," called a man one day,
"I've been working so long on my writing,
I'd love to know what you might have to say,
I hope you will find it quite exciting."

The author's talent was the only theme,
boasting, bragging, (It was awful, really!)
At last he seemed to have run out of steam,
"Dear Master," he intoned, "Please speak freely."

Aesop was annoyed by all this nonsense,
he could not complete the asked-for review,
saying, "Your need for praise is quite intense,
Praise yourself, no one will do it for you."

Study your trade with a fine master
or your work may be a disaster.

Fox Sees Clearly

Seeing a lion for the first time,
a fox was so frightened that he ran.
He said, "I'll avoid him if I can,
or I'll die in fear, though he's sublime."

Next day the fox saw the noble beast
holding court, smoking his pipe, at ease,
thought, "Why, he reminds me of calm seas,
perhaps I should show myself, at least."

Hoping to make things better, not worse,
he got up his courage, wound his way.
He approached and called, "Dear King, good day."
The lion beamed, "Hi, there. Let's converse."

First impressions may give a poor view,
seek beyond looks to find what is true.

The Four Oxen and the Lion

Each time the lion made an attack,
the four oxen would turn, touching tails,
facing the lion who then drew back
as the oxen stood firm, and laughed gales.

When the oxen had a falling out,
they parted, feuding, each went his way.
The lion's job was merely to clout
them one by one. They were quite easy prey.

Stay closely united
when villains are sighted.

The Horse and the Stag

A simple horse had been the master
of a lovely clearing in the wood,
but a mean stag had caused a disaster,
ripping turf, running as fast as he could.

The horse begged a soldier, "Please help me,
this wild beast is destroying my home."
"Of course, just try this bit and you'll see,
together we'll force the stag to roam."

The horse guessed, "The bit helps to be brave,"
the soldier mounted, added the rein;
at once the horse knew he was a slave,
the stag took off, he had only pain.

Helpers who lay down conditions
get folks into strange positions.

5554-MURP

Raven and Swallow

Raven and Swallow met for high tea,
"I'm getting rather tired, you see,
having my feathers adored on me,"
said Swallow in a manner queenly.

"That well may be so, dear," Raven cawed,
"It's a small thing to be admired.
In winter I'm warmly attired
by my black feathers, worthy of laud."

The birds exchanged some lady-like slams,
about admirers and themselves,
till Raven asked, "Time for tea and jams?"
Swallow took down goodies from her shelves.

Most people will find it's quite a good deal
to stop arguing, enjoy a fine meal.

The Dog That Loved Eggs

"Is it real? This is lucky for me,"
crooned softly the dog that so loved eggs,
(at the big table on his hind legs,)
looked at a bowl of white shells, "I see

"My heart's desire, I'll eat the lot,
it will be my very own dream feast,
I have no restraint, I'm just a beast."
He swallowed the biggest, like a shot.

His stomach felt heavy, "Oh, such pain,
now I know that all things round and white
are not good, look at me, what a sight;
if I live I'll try to use my brain."

Be sure to look before you leap,
or you may end up in a heap.

Town Mouse, Country Mouse

"You dare call this a meal?" squeaked Town Mouse,
in his friend's wreck of a country house,
"Old roots and bulbs are hardly good food,
come to town, we'll be in a fine mood."

Town Mouse guaranteed him gourmet fare,
"Delicious scraps your palate shall tease,
honey, beans, cream and eggs, if you please."
Country Mouse agreed, off went the pair.

They praised the gilded dining table
and sat down before the splendid spread.
Scared by a maid, ran fast as able,
through the Great Hall and under a bed.

Twice more alarmed, with no chance to eat,
Country Mouse gasped, "I'm feeling the heat,
the only course for me is retreat
to home for roots, for dessert, a beet.

Simple food may not have the best taste,
but who can eat well when being chased?

Stick Together

A man, upset by his sons' constant fighting,
called them together to halt recurring strife.
"This lesson, my sons, may not be exciting,
but it will show you something I've learned in life."

He gave each son a stick and ordered, "Break it,"
which they accomplished quickly, in the same way,
then said, "Break these bundles," but soon they all quit.
"Let me summarize then, my sons, if I may,

"Fight one another, you'll be prey to all men,
stay close together and you'll always be strong,
vow never to fight with your brothers again
and you'll be unbeatable your whole life long."

Equality Takes Time

A hunt party, donkey, lion , fox,
relaxed at camp to divide their catch.
Lion growled, "Donkey — some in each box."
He did so, each amount a match.

The lion, angry, then punched him out,
spoke, "Now fox, you make a decision,
I hope you know what this is about."
The fox made a prudent division.

To the lion, he gave most booty,
to himself, only the slightest bit.
The lion smiled, "You've done your duty,
you see things clearly. Let's eat now. Sit."

Joining lions for dinner
can make you thinner

5554-MURP

Hear the Sea

A shipwrecked sailor swam safely to shore,
fell, quite exhausted by the raging sea.
Next day he said, "Now it's my turn to roar,
"Water, take shame for what you did to me."

The sea cried, "Wait, you do me a great wrong,
my nature is peaceful, as you see now,
it's the wind that sings that loud, fearful song,
I'd like to resist, but I don't know how."

Go very slowly, almost to a halt,
be extra sure before assigning fault.

War Over

A horse carried his master when he battled,
was called 'Hero Horse' when sabres were rattled,
he was fed the best food that could be procured,
thought that this treatment was forever assured.

The war was over, he returned to the farm,
there treated like a slave, exposed to all harm,
had big loads to move, pulling wagons all day,
for food had leftovers, and maybe some hay.

Then war came again and he was saddled up,
his master thought he was lively as a pup,
but being too weak, he said, "I have no steam,
may I suggest you join the Foot Soldiers Team!"

Poor performance is expected
if your assets are neglected.

Winter vs. Spring

Winter patronized Spring, "Listen, my dear,
it is well-known that each time you appear,
people run to fields, to woods and to streams,
picking flowers, watching birds, living dreams.

"Some leave home, some travel to odd places,
some are quite mad to look at new faces
and do a million things that create din,
and worst of all, they avoid discipline.

"When I'm in charge, folks are calm and steady,
can stand foul weather, are ever ready
to bear my hardships, as I think they should.
By the way, I'd end your reign, if I could."

Spring spoke, "There may be truth in what you say,
I know they miss me when I've gone away,
they check their calendars, long for my date,
sound my name with gladness and smile and wait,

"Till I breathe life into a tired world,
bring blue heavens, warmth and flowers unfurled.
In my own way I do have fine order,
and it's my turn now, please cross time's border."

A Friendly Visit

Chatty Cat came to visit Sick Hen,
peppered her with questions unnerving,
"Where did you get this illness? And when?
Is it bad? This is all disturbing,

"There must be something for which you yearn,
What is it? Are you better? Please tell."
"Thank you Ms. Cat for your concern,
feel free to leave, I'll be quickly well."

It makes a person go round the bend,
listening to chatter without end.

83

Keep Focused

An artistic goat studied a rock,
causing him to lose touch with his flock.
Then, moving homeward at a slow pace,
suddenly was standing face to face
with a wolf. He improvised,

"Please don't eat me yet, first let me dance,
you play the flute, my art to enhance,"
and the wolf most graciously complied,
tootling his very best at the side
of the dancing goat.

The music's strains brought a pack of dogs,
the goat ran and hid behind some logs,
the wolf howled, "I left my butcher's work
to be a musician. What a quirk!"

You may not get hurt
if you learn to divert.

Friendship Laid Bare

Walking together, an amiable pair,
who, before it saw them, had spotted a bear.
One ran fast, hid in a tree, afraid to stay,
the other was slow, could not run away,
so he decided it was best to play dead,
and the bear began to sniff him, foot to head.

The man believed that bears leave the dead alone,
he held his breath, avoided sounding a moan.
The bear departed, the friend leaped from the tree,
asking, "Did the bear say anything of me?"
"Oh, yes. He said 'A friend becomes a stranger
who deserts and hides in the face of danger'."

Call that person a friend
who will stay till the end.

Outfoxed

A mean, old fox, relaxing one day,
observed a young crow flying away
with a piece of cheese held in her beak
and said, "That appears worthwhile to seek,"
and followed the crow.

He ambled to her tree, head held high,
began to smile, looked her in the eye
and crooned, "Lady Crow, please let me say
how glossy your feathers are today,
you are a queen among birds.

"The truth is your voice is sweet and clear,
please sing a soft song for me, my dear."
Her beak opened to sing her 'CAW' song,
she suddenly knew something was wrong
as the cheese hit the ground.

The fox smiled slyly, laughed, "That will do,
the cheese was all I wanted from you,
I must advise you, in all matters,
beware the creature that flatters,"
and the crow pitied the fox.

P.S.   Much later she heard that he was sick
and flew to him with a piece of meat.
Astonished by the crow's gracious feat,
he promised to give up his old trick.

The Lion and
the Woodsman's Daughter

Madly in love, a mighty lion
demanded a beauty for his bride.
Her father said, "I am no scion,
but I vow I'll set this beast aside."

He told the lion his daughter feared
big claws and big teeth. She'd love him if
they were removed, he could keep his beard.
The lion agreed, "There'll be no tiff."

Done! The father, holding the trump card,
told the lion, "The game is over,
be sure to avoid eating what's hard,
from now on you'll be gumming clover."

Take what you want, show you're tough;
you may find the going rough.

The Bald Truth

A man with hair that was partly gray,
had two lady friends, one young, one old,
he liked them both, but could not say
which one for a lifetime he would hold.

The old one thought he looked much too young,
so she pulled out all hair that was black,
the young one removed gray hair that hung,
she thought that would make the years roll back.

Both ladies chose to drop him when he was hairless,
saying, "He's not handsome, we just couldn't care less."

I've heard it said that love is blind;
that's not usual, you will find.

Wolves and Sheep with Dogs Gone

The Wolf Council came to see the sheep,
"We're all for peace, we're tired of wars,
the only ones who gain are those bores,
the big and ugly dogs that you keep."

"If that is all," spoke the Sheep Congress,
"We can dismiss them, they boss us too,
perhaps this will clean a sorry mess,
and we'll be good neighbors with you."

The dogs were fired, moved out of town,
the wolves said, "Now we're part of your crowd."
In a short time, the sheep were put down,
many disappeared, others were cowed.

Beware of well-meaning 'friends',
they probably have their own ends.

Bees, Drones and Wasp

As usual, the busy bees built a comb
while the lazy drones just hung around and watched.
Strangely, the drones then claimed they had made the home.
The bees buzzed, "This fabrication must be scotched."

They went to court to fight, Judge Wasp presiding,
he listened to all arguments of the case.
He spoke, "This is difficult in deciding,
my tasting honey, it seems, shall be its base.

"Let each group now fashion a new place to dwell,
I'll taste honey from each to find which has won
when compared with the first. I shall decide well,
and in an instant or two, we will be done."

The worker bees whirred, "YES, that will surely please,"
the drowsy drones hummed, "Noooooo, this is much too
tough."
The judge knew the truth, ruled quickly for the bees,
he called out, "Let there be no more droning guff."

There are many fakers
but few great homemakers.

The Young Fox's Tale

A bold, young fox was told, "Without fail
stay near the pack! The safe place to be."
He went into the woods, lost his tail
struggling from a trap he didn't see.

Fearing his friends would make fun of him,
thought, "I'll sway them to cut theirs off too."
He said, "Like me, you'll be full of vim,
you'll jump higher, run faster, it's true."

"First, we're not laughing, it's rather sad,
but it's not as bad as being dead,
we're not going to cut ours off, lad,
start living your life," the Head Fox said.

If you try to fake it out,
you'll create a lot of doubt.

5554-MURP

The Tree and the Reed

"Stand tall, little one," said tree to reed,
a little backbone is what you need,
raise your head up high, take my lead,
you want folks to think you're a weed?"

"You're really strong," reed began to squeak,
"By my nature, I'm a little weak,
going with the flow is what I seek,
please forgive my boldness when I speak."

A wild hurricane began to blow,
the tree was felled quickly, even though
it fought hard. The reed said, "Now I know
bending to the wind can prevent woe."

If life's winds say, "You are next,"
try to stay a little flexed.

Hares and Frogs

Nervous wrecks, thinking that they would fall
into traps their foes perhaps could make,
the hares decided to end it all
by jumping into a nearby lake.

Reaching the lake's banks, they could see
nervous frogs jumping into the deep.
A hare said, "What! They're more scared than we.
Let's live; but live like lions, not sheep."

When things go wrong, don't despair,
everyone has things to bear.

5554-MURP

Use or Lose

A wealthy old man sold all that he had,
bought many gold bars and buried them deep,
daily visits there for years made him glad,
he'd rather be near them than eat or sleep.

Watching him, a gardener guessed the treasure,
unearthed it unseen and ran far away,
the miser was saddened beyond measure,
a friend saw his misery, came to say,

"Why not take a stone, put it in the ground,
replacing the gold which you never used,
it will serve as well as the bars you downed
and your anxiety will be defused."

Life is much too short,
get yourself a sport.

A Meal Denied

A boar and a lion, slowed by thirst,
found a cool stream shaded from the sun,
they argued an hour who should drink first
and vowed to fight until there was one.

Then they saw flying high in the sky
vultures waiting for the fight to start.
This caused them to call the fight a tie,
to drink their fill and, as friends, to part.

Pride can come before a fall,
share and you'll be standing tall.

The Bat, The Birds and The Beasts

Another great war was about to begin,
a bat considered which of two groups would win,
"Should I join the birds? All know they are clever.
Or the beasts? They'll be strong in this endeavor."

"Come to us," said the birds. "Can't! Beast I may be."
He told the beasts, "I'm a bird. I think. I'll see."
He thought and continued to equivocate.
Peace quickly was made, signing up was too late.

He wanted to join the birds' celebration;
they hooted, "You're not part of our fine nation."
He thought, "The others will welcome me, at least,"
but beasts' interest in him had quickly ceased.

If you want to go far
you must know who you are.

Retired Hen

A well-known hen was wont to say,
"My eggs are perfect, one each day."
Her mistress took a greedy view,
"Why have one when you can have two?"

She gave the hen a double feed
which, in fact, was a stupid deed.
The hen grew fat, from spring to fall,
and never gave more eggs at all.

Greedy changes are not wise,
you soon can lose what you prize.

No Thanks

Chased by some hunters, a frightened fox asked for aid.
"To my hut," called a woodsman, "To avoid this raid."
The hunters came, asked if he'd seen a fox pass by,
he said, "No," but wanting to show that this was a lie,
he looked toward the hut.

They missed his message, left, the fox started to leave,
the woodsman spoke, "Thanks are in order, I believe."
The fox's words were sharp, "I was grateful to you,
but you tried to betray me, only shame is due,"
and the woodsman turned away.

If you want people's praise
you must have honest ways.

Across the Water

Wounded painfully from blows he took,
victim of a battle with a dog,
a wolf lay quietly in a bog
when he saw a sheep across a brook.

"Sheep, I am helpless. Please bring a drink,
that's all I want, I'll get my own meat."
The sheep thought it over, gave a bleat,
"I'm not as dumb as a wolf may think."

Underestimating the weak
may not get you all that you seek.

The Fox and the Lion

A lion and a fox had hunted all day,
The fox spoke, "Let's eat our catch without delay."
The lion roared, "Leave that dead donkey alone,
"I'll take a nap and later you'll get a bone."

The lion left, the fox ate the donkey's brains,
he was unable to hold back hunger's reins.
The lion woke, yawned, then came right back to see
that the brains had been removed from the donkey.

He told the fox, "You're in a bad position,
the donkey's brainless, explain that condition!"
The fox said, "He never had brains as he ought,
or the poor, dumb beast would never have been caught."

Fooling a king isn't so easy,
try it, you'll find you can get queasy.

Delusion Abounds but Talent is Rare

With a voice subdued as a delicate flower,
an aspiring singer drilled at home by the hour.
Because the high tile walls produced a mighty sound,
he believed that his voice was powerfully round.

He hired a theater to flaunt his talent,
the audience listened and away they all went,
the front rows soon reacted with a loud catcall
and the back rows could not hear his light voice at all.

Don't think yourself extraordinary
if evidence is to the contrary.

5554-MURP

A Friend in Need

A hare felt popular and secure
because the other beasts declared, "Sure,
you're one of us until forever,
nothing in this world can sever
our relationship."

One day she heard the hounds assembling ,
went to the dray horse, said while trembling,
"Please carry me far away from here."
"Can't," he spoke, "I've work to do, my dear,
try the bull."

She thought the bull's horns would chase the hounds,
he said, "The ladies demand my rounds,
try the goat."

The goat, well-known as a great actor,
lied, "Can't run, says my chiropractor,
try the ram."
The ram balked, "I'd love to work this feat
but those hungry hounds also want us to eat,
try the calf ."

She exclaimed, "Heavens, how could you ask,
you can see I'm too young for this task,
and the hounds are near."
Having no one on whom to rely,
the hare ran fast as a bird can fly
and escaped the hounds.

The Dog, the Rooster and the Fox

Friends dog and rooster, wandering, went
in the woods till they could hardly see,
they hadn't prepared, they had no tent,
they made their beds in a nearby tree.

The rooster woke, gave his daily crow,
a fox smiled, "Is this my breakfast treat?
"You have a lovely voice, come below
from the high branches, so we can meet."

The rooster thought the fox a villain,
knew the dog slept in the tree below,
called, "Knock, my doorman will let you in,"
the fox knocked and the dog laid him low.

Be careful seeking forbidden booty,
there may be a big dog on duty.

Sour Grapes

Mister Hungry Fox looked up to see
juicy grapes on a vine in a tree
and said to himself, "They are for me,
if only like a giraffe I'll be."

He stretched his big paws to their full height
but couldn't reach the grapes, what a plight!,
left annoyed, saying , with teeth held tight,
"No way they'll ripen in a fortnight."

Cheer up lads, smile each hour,
life's too short to stay sour.

A Blind Man Sees

A blind man in a distant hamlet
had a gift that caused many a bet,
he knew each beast put into his hands,
identified all from distant lands.

A baby wolf was brought by the mob,
they bet this time he'd have a tough job,
"Fox or wolf, not sure, (They had a shock)
but when he grows, keep him from your flock."

Those, by blindness set apart,
can often cut to the heart.

Lion, Bear and Fox

A strong lion and a big, old bear
came upon the carcass of a sheep,
they fought fiercely to see who would keep
it, but collapsed, an exhausted pair.

A crafty fox trotted to the scene,
he checked things out, then left with the meat,
The lion spoke, "We fought but he'll eat.
Next time let's be more mature, old bean."

Some learn late from incidents untoward,
cooperation has its own reward.

Large and Small, Same Rights for All

A beautiful forest in the fall,
a woodcutter begs the elder trees,
"A little piece of wood, if you please,
my ax needs a handle, that is all."

They discussed at great length his request,
not wanting to do anything rash,
thought to give him a smaller, young ash,
stated that this course might be the best.

The woodsman made his handle, started
to chop down trees, every age and sort,
no one could stop him, no judge, no court,
and the elder trees were down-hearted.

"What fools we were to give him assent,
to rule that the young ash might not grow,
who survives must let the whole world know
the rights of the small must not be bent."

Making decisions that might cause a fall,
perhaps should have the agreement of all.

Pig Will Out

A lonely pig that had been roaming about,
met some sheep and a goat and he grazed with them.
Their shepherd came, his hungry look left no doubt
that he had made some plans for this porcine gem.

The pig spoke, "There's danger," the sheep baaaed, "Relax."
The goat said, "He likes us and scratches our backs."
Squealed the pig, "Your fine wool makes up your appeal,
but what he sees in me is a hearty meal."

When it's clear you may grieve,
it's more than time to leave.

117

The Cat and the Prince

A cat fell in love with a handsome Prince,
she knew that to win him she must convince
the Local Fairy to make her a girl
and set the Prince's head in a whirl.

The Fairy kindly approved this appeal,
made the cat beautiful, blindingly real.
The Prince met the girl and he lost his heart
and they were wed, said that they'd never part.

Soon the Fairy wondered if the Princess
had changed quite fully and now did possess
all human qualities, without a doubt,
so she designed a test to find that out.

She placed a mouse in the palace at night,
the Princess, on all fours, grabbed, took a bite.
The Prince fainted, dropping his glass of wine,
The Fairy changed the Princess to feline.

If you want to change, you can win
but you must show some discipline.

The Tortoise and the Birds

A tortoise was bored with her dwelling,
she decided to move far away,
asked an eagle to fly her, telling
him she would present him with good pay.

Off they flew, met a crow who cawed low,
"Eagle, the tortoise is good eating,"
the eagle said, "Shell is too hard, go
away, I must keep these wings beating."

"Those big things below," said crow, "Are rocks!"
The eagle grasped the concept's appeal,
he dropped the poor tortoise near the docks
and the birds enjoyed a tasty meal.

When choosing a mover, take care,
you want someone who'll get you there.

5554-MURP

The Fisherman's Flute

A flute-playing fisherman had the thought
to make fish dance into his net on shore
by playing his music for those he sought
who'd come to him happily by the score.

He played many tunes but no fish appeared,
discouraged, he threw his net to the sea
and was amazed, he even thought it weird
that so many came out so willingly.

In the net, the fish jumped and flopped about,
as all fish will do when no longer free.
"Don't dance now," the flutist said with a pout,
"When I played, you refused to dance for me."

No matter how hard you blow,
fantasizing won't make it so.

Wolf and Lion

A wolf, at night, smelled a flock of sheep,
stole a lamb, escaped without a peep.
He had run close to his secret lair
when a lion jumped and caught the pair.

Wolf said, "Let go, there'll be no dealing,
taking him is not right, it's stealing."
Lion laughed, "RIGHT? You haven't a clue,
I doubt the shepherd gave him to you!"

If you steal and then one from you steals,
don't apply to the Court of Appeals.

One Good Trick Deserves Another

A merchant loaded salt onto his donkey
which promptly stumbled and fell into a creek,
some salt then melted, as other salt ran free,
his big load was lighter, his life not as bleak.

They went back to town, the man, feeling tension,
loaded more salt and had it packed very tight.
The beast fell, but this time it was his intention,
he knew well that his big load would soon be light.

Annoyed, now aware his donkey was lax,
the merchant, to punish him, contrived a plot.
He loaded large sponges, ignoring salt sacks,
judging sponges full of water weighed a lot.

They marched together to the very same place,
down went the donkey, he got up slowly, then
the weight of soaked sponges brought shock to his face,
he never tried to trick his master again.

Be careful improving work conditions,
any changes can arouse suspicions.

The Fox and the Crane

A comical fox, (or so he thought),
invited a crane to share a meal.
To prepare, there was little food bought,
which a glance at table would reveal.

The fox put soup in a shallow dish,
asked the crane, "Won't you take a part?"
The crane, embarrassed, try as he wish,
could not lap, just wet his bill. Not smart

of the fox to ask, "Don't like the soup?"
In a great huff, crane began to plan
a meal that would soon make the fox droop.
He invited him, "Come when you can."

At the crane's he found a long-necked jar,
he got no soup through its narrow mouth.
Crane smiled, "How do you like it so far?"
Conceding, fox cried, "I'm heading south."

Be nasty in life and you can bet,
a double nasty is what you'll get.

127

Singer's Choice

A bird in a cage sang only at night,
a bat wondered if she too hated light,
"Why is it that you do not sing by day?
Isn't that for you the usual way?"
asked the curious bat.

The bird answered, I was singing one morn
when suddenly from my tree I was torn,
put in a cage and this has been my lot,
I learned a lesson I never forgot,
It's dangerous to sing by day."

"My dear little bird, my friend in the night,
you surely are in a difficult plight,
but permit me to say, about your fate,
maybe you have learned your lesson too late,
or hadn't you noticed?"

Put failure behind you,
Don't let it blind you.

The Mischievous Dog

A mischievous dog used to sneak up on all
and give each a bite without any warning.
His master decided this cast such a pall
that he thought to buy a large bell one morning.

He put the bell in place around the dog's neck,
so all the animals knew he was nearby.
Life for everyone was no longer a wreck
but the dog grew proud of his bell and would try

to ring it loudly to the town's vexation,
until an old fox drew him roughly aside,
"Foolish dog, the bell is your condemnation,
your notice that you have good manners defied."

Bad behavior is often taken for fame,
would-be celebrities like to play this game.

Top Mother

The forest beasts lacked things to discuss;
found a topic that caused a twitter,
they questioned themselves, "Tell, who of us
had the most offspring in a litter?"

Some shouted loudly, "I had many,"
some knew they had no child songs to sing.
They asked a lioness, "Lots? Any? "
She smiled, "Just one. But he is a King."

Some say, ' No', others will agree,
quality over quantity.

Reason to Crow

Seeking water, a thirsty crow
spotted a pitcher, thin and tall,
looked inside, saw water below,
but he could not reach it at all.

Worn out from thinking what to do,
he gave up hope, sat down and cried;
saw pebbles which gave him a clue,
"What would happen if they're inside . . . ?"

The crow dropped the stones, one by one,
into his pitcher, watched them sink,
and by and by when he was done,
water had surfaced, he had his drink.

Don't give up hoping,
you'll soon be coping.

Stick to Business

A frightened donkey saw a wolf one day.
Thinking quickly he said, "Help, I am lame."
The nosy wolf asked how he got that way,
"At play, this thorn in my hoof is to blame.

"You should pull it out before you eat me,
it could cut your mouth and you'll be depressed."
Wolf checked the hoof of the examinee,
wanting the donkey at his very best.

The donkey swiftly gave a mighty kick,
the wolf lost his teeth, said in contrition,
"If my father saw me he'd be sick,
he raised a butcher, not a physician."

When you find yourself in a stew,
thinking may be the thing for you.

The Workman and the Nightingale

A nightingale sang her sweet song through the night,
a workman was charmed by the music he heard,
he wanted to possess the beautiful bird,
so he trapped her and caged her, without a fight.

The workman said, "Now you will sing just for me."
She chirped, "Nightingales don't sing in cages."
"I'll eat you then, haven't had bird in ages."
She offered, "Three things worth gold, if I'm set free."

He let her out, the bird said, "One – Don't believe
a captive's promise; Two – keep what you have got;
Three – Of things lost forever, accept your lot.
Don't be bitter. Learn kindness. I take my leave."

To be all that you can be,
man or bird, you must be free.

Dog Gone

A scrawny dog, having a quick nap
in the sun, by the water tower,
woke to behold a very bad chap,
Mr. Wolf, gripping him with power,
and thought fast.

The dog looked into those hungry eyes
and saw that there was no time to waste.
He smiled, "For you I have a surprise,
eat me later, I'll have a good taste."
The wolf said, "Go on..."

"I'm on my way to a big wedding,
I'll eat great foods and be rich eating."
"You may go, but better be heading
back or I'll give you a beating."

NEXT DAY

"COME DOWN DOG, off that tower. "I'm shocked!"
"Not a chance, this is my new station.
If you see me below," the dog mocked,
"Please don't wait for a celebration,"
and the wolf slinked away.

Hold on to good stuff
or you will be gruff.

Treasure Found

A farmer, quite ill, wanted to share
his knowledge with both his lazy sons,
how the soil is tilled, how a farm runs,
how the two could be a working pair.

But he was wise to downplay this part,
said only, "I leave you my treasure,
which is in the fields, beyond measure,"
and they ran to work with horse and cart.

They ploughed for gold. (A servant threw seed,
unknown to them.) Their search did not stop.
At summer's end there was a great crop,
they saw they had all the wealth they'd need.

Use of time is a test,
take care where you invest.

5554-MURP

Mr. Frog, M.D.

A frog croaked, "Fellow swamp dwellers, HEAR,
I've studied medicine for a year,
I'm ready to cure all diseases
for just a small fee, if it pleases."

A doubtful fox questioned frog's knowledge,
"Model please what you learned in college,
First – Straighten your, ugly, wrinkled skin,
show us how to fix your walk...Begin!"

If you can't cure yourself
Doctor, stay on the shelf.

141

The Fox and the Cat

Fox told cat, "I must say I'm clever,
I've many ways of not getting caught."
The cat mewed, "Lucky you, I've never
had but one, "Up a tree," mother taught.

The hounds were approaching where they stood,
the cat took right off, zoomed up a tree;
The fox thought, "Perhaps I could or should
do this or that, h-m- m-m, now let me see."

From her place quite high, the cat observed
the fox and hounds, in a collision.
Fox cried, "Help, I'm totally unnerved,
Woe! I just can't make a decision."

Given choices, good to best,
choose any one, leave the rest.

The Lion Takes Counsel

A lion called a sheep to query,
"Give me the truth now, does my breath smell?"
"The worst," said a sheep, "Awful, dearie."
"Get out," growled the King, "If you'd stay well."

He summoned a wolf and asked the same,
"The sweetest breath," wolf lied, "of the lot."
"LIAR, be gone, you've nothing but shame.
Let's look around, who else have we got?"

Next he called out for a fox to tell,
(The beast ranks were getting thinner,)
"I have a bad cold, I cannot smell."
"O.K., fox," King said, "Stay for dinner."

Ignorance can be wise,
if sound health you prize.

5554-MURP

Family History

The other animals watched with glee
    at the mule that pretended to be,
"A star race horse, just like my mother,
watch me run around like no other."

He was lively, had plenty of pride;
next day though, he showed another side.
Quite worn out, (he'd been loaded with tasks),
    "My dad's a donkey, if anyone asks."

Don't let others put you down,
take your lumps, then go to town.

Wolf Down

A greyish wolf with little appeal,
walking in search of a late day meal.
His shadow now grew, to his surprise,
an unexpected increase in size.

Soon it lengthened to such a degree,
he howled, "No one is bigger than me,
now I'm the boss of all I survey,
lions and hunters, out of my way."

A lion appeared, looking quite lean,
one could see he was hungry and mean.
He thought the wolf looked big as a pup,
ignored the shadow, swallowed him up.

If suddenly you are greater than all,
you may need to give your doctor a call.

The Bowman and the Lion

A man of skill with bow and arrow
was seen in the forest on the hunt;
animals ran, chilled to the marrow,
a large lion challenged, strong and blunt,

"I'll fight!" The bowman said, "My respect,
let my messenger help you decide."
He loosed an arrow with quick effect,
it found its mark in the lion's side.

"Why'd you quit?" a teary fox implored,
I thought at least you'd give a sharp strike."
"Tough messenger," lion said, I am floored.
What can the HUNTER's power be like?"

If you'd like to see another day,
know when it's your turn to step away.

If Lions Could Build

An unusual pair strolled in the forest,
a man and a lion, each having his say,
each boasting his strength, said that put to the test,
he would win the battle and carry the day.

As tempers flared, they saw a statue nearby,
a beaten lion, a man's foot on its chest;
the man shouted, "You see, the facts do not lie,
of all known fighters, surely man is the best."

The lion smiled, "Such are the tales men invent,
then build statues representing each tale's flaw;
if lions could build such, no truth would be bent,
you'd see many men under that lion's paw."

Whether old or still in youth,
men may tend to stretch the truth.

5554-MURP

The Donkey and the Lion Skin

A donkey found an old lion skin,
put it right on, pretended to be
a mighty lion so he could win
attention from all living calmly

in the forest. The donkey, amused
as he scared all beasts and watched them run,
did not roar which had them all confused,
he chuckled quietly, had his fun.

He spied a fox and moved very near,
made a sound. The fox laughed, "Near or far,
a lion that brays does not cause fear,
I know you for the donkey you are."

Impersonation is really an art,
beginners must study before they start.

The Old Man and Death

An old man paused, weary as could be,
from carrying a big pile of wood.
In despair, he said, "Death, come for me,
I can't get up, if only I could."

The old man was shocked when Death appeared,
asking, "Can I help, are you ready?"
"Not exactly, please don't think me weird,
help me with my wood, I'm not steady."

When death calls, be ready to go,
if you call him, that's another show.

Crane Checked

A wolf ran to a crane and managed to shout,
"There's a big bone in my throat, please take it out,
I'll pay you anything, whatever you wish."
The crane agreed and thought he'd ask for some fish.

His long bill extracted the bone in a flash.
He said, "I'll take fifteen fish, I don't want cash."
"The reward," laughed the wolf, "Is that you contrived
to put your head in my mouth and you survived."

Informal contracts, it's said, can have flaws,
for instance – when one party has big jaws.

5554-MURP

The Rooster and the Pearl

A rooster was marching, head held high,
surveying his barnyard, full of self,
when, in a pile of straw, near a shelf,
something round and shiny caught his eye.

He approached, leaned over, scratched a bit,
poked around and uncovered a pearl,
"Probably lost," he thought, "By some girl,
the thing interests me not a whit."

"I'd rather have a big piece of corn
than this 'treasure' of dim-witted men,"
he confided to a nearby hen.
"Now, back to work on a lovely morn."

Each has his/her own measure
to decide what's treasure.